NOTES FOR LIGHTING A FIRE

Also by Gerry Cambridge:

Aves, Essence Press, 2007
Madame Fi Fi's Farewell and Other Poems, Luath Press, 2003
The Praise of Swans, Shoestring Press, 2000
*'Nothing But Heather!': Scottish Nature in Poems,
Photographs and Prose,* Luath Press, 1999
The Shell House, Scottish Cultural Press, 1995
The Dark Gift and Other Poems, St Inans Press, 1994

NOTES FOR LIGHTING
A FIRE

Gerry Cambridge

Happen*Stance*

© Gerry Cambridge 2012, 2013
ISBN 978-1-905939-96-1
All rights reserved.

Notes for Lighting a Fire was first published in hard cover in 2012. This is a revised edition with five additional poems, first issued 2013, reprinted 2016 and 2019.

The author gratefully acknowledges the Bursary Panel of the then Scottish Arts Council in 2009 for its award of a writing bursary that enabled the completion of this collection, John Hudson for his co-ordination of a writing residency at Au Diable Vauvert and Montpellier in May, 2004, and the Royal Literary Fund for its support.

Thanks to the editors of the following, in which poems from this collection, sometimes in earlier versions, first appeared: *Chapman, Island, The Hudson Review, Markings, The New Shetlander, Northwords Now, Poetry Review, Textualities*; and the anthologies *Stepping into the Avalanche* (Brownsbank Press, 2003), *Winter Gifts* (HappenStance Press, 2004), *Speaking English* (Five Leaves Poetry, 2007), and *For Angus: Poems, Prose, Sketches and Music*, a memorial volume for the poet and historian Angus Calder (Los Poetry Press, 2009). 'Anthotype' was commissioned in 2010 by the Edinburgh artist Nicola Murray for a project involving this process; 'Minimalist' was set as a limited edition linocut by the Scottish artist Hilke MacIntyre, as part of a collaboration between Edinburgh Printmakers and the Scottish Poetry Library in 2013.

Thanks also to early readers of the typescript for critical feedback: Diana Hendry, Julie Kane, Rob A. Mackenzie, James McGonigal, Marcia Menter and N.S. Thompson.

Printed and bound by Imprint Digital, Exeter
https://digital.imprint.co.uk

Published in 2013 by HappenStance
21 Hatton Green, Glenrothes, Fife KY7 4SD
www.happenstancepress.com

CONTENTS

I

Notes for Lighting a Fire / 11
Processional / 12
Little Light Psalm / 13
Two Chirps at Mid-Winter / 14
Young Snow / 15
Blowing Out an Egg / 16
Sacrifice / 17
A Sparrowhawk's Nest / 18
The Herriers / 19
At Twelve / 20
The Whitethroat at Hamilton Bus Station / 21

II

Light Up Lanarkshire / 25
Light Leaves (1):
   i / 30
   ii / 31
   iii / 32
   iv / 33
   v / 34
   vi / 35
   vii / 36
   viii / 37
   ix / 38
   x / 39
Exposure / 40
Anthotype / 41

III

Christmas Oranges / 45
Praise of a Winter Solstice / 46
Minimalist / 47
Gorse in Middle Age / 48
Progress / 49
In Irvine / 50
Find / 51
Shell Beach, Eigg / 52
Light Leaves (2) :
    i / 54
    ii / 55
Take-off / 56
The Lesson / 57
Awakening / 58
Frog City / 60
The Queen / 61
Alight / 62
'Hearing Astronomers Speak' / 63
Stylophilia / 64
Retreat / 65
The Great Things / 66
That Dusk / 68

In memory of
Brendan Joseph Cambridge

ORDER
for B. J. C.

Up to the things of day, old man,
up like the sun, for a briefer time;
up to the kettle, up to the table,
to the tiny kitchen of yellow rays
jewelling the breakfast crumbs.
Here is your shaver. Keep at bay
the daily push to rank disorder for
as long as you are able.

Love is left in spite of all
your sins and weaknesses have been—
not huge, by the world's black heights.

Wash your face again with common water, though
the star that lifts and gifts this day
is night on your world's side.

I

Notes for Lighting a Fire

First, clean the ash from the grate.
Fetch the metal bucket from the outhouse
under the bitter glint of the winter stars.
Your steps crunch on the frosting gravel.
The universe tonight at this height above sea-level
feels like a vast deep freeze. Scrape
of metal on metal and stone as you shovel
the ash back to a clean beginning.
Prepare the papers. Broadsheets are best.
Diagonally roll the last week's news, disasters, crimes,
twist each roll in a circle, and tuck the ends in.
Place half a dozen of these in the metal grate.
Then the kindling—bought sticks or, better,
twigs and slim branches the gales brought down
in the pine wood. Lay them across the papers.
Fill the coal scuttle from the slumped heavy sack.
The biggest coals to the bottom, mind,
for the established fire; smaller coals to the top.
Place these fastidiously about on the kindling
like punctuation, and light each paper twist's
edge with a match. Watch the living orange lick and feed.
Hopefully it will catch. Add more coal when needed
till the heart of the blaze is incandescent
and the room fills up with ambient warmth;
so the task, but for tipping chunks from the scuttle
occasionally, is done. Now you can settle
to the scratch of a pen in praise of primordial fire
with its lapping sound, as earth in its tilt turning round
swings Orion up sparking like a spaceship
of light from behind the black burial mound of that hill.

Processional

He has gone down into darkness at the wrecked end of the year
And is lying, gaberlunzie, in the needled nest of frost.
The arctic thrushes call for him although he cannot hear,

And the worm too understands him in the freeze-grip of its dark,
And the ptarmigan in blizzards where no thought is worth a crumb,
And treecreepers in shivering puffs in Wellingtonias' bark.

Shop windows glint in city lights like ice and sky, but still
No tinsel gifts can touch him, freed to silence like a stone's;
His face is white as paper's white in miles-high midnight chill.

He lies as plain as frost-dust where those starving thrushes call,
And his lime and ray-struck armoury could hardly be less small
On the anvil of beginnings in the sun's gate on the wall.

Little Light Psalm
21st December

Glaurlight.
  Dankpuddlelight; light
poor as a dosser's pocket.
  Duskalldaylight
too drab to praise as grey.
  Light the diamond
lost in the mine;
  light divine
in the older way.

Spacelight.
  Light of celandine;
pollenlight
sudden in faces.
  Jaywinglight—its turquoise
flash. Light
  of the May. Keylight turning
  in the ash of dawn,
loosening seizedlight
  on this grim day.

Two Chirps at Mid-Winter

I

To think of the crystal of snow: as if
   Hammered in permanent silver, though
     Perfectly evanescent:
The blueprint, immortal, of the butterfly wing:
   Each ferned inscription of the frost. To think
Of the principles that exist beyond their object,
   Plato's ethereal diamond.
     Ark in perpetual rain,
Such thoughts that are like lanterns
   Immutably shining in immutable dark.

II

In the blank perfection of snow descending,
That was unifying the wide
Intricate landscape back to an un-nibbed page,
I stood with the two great Clydesdales. They blew
Oven-breath through vibrating lips and shook
Their granite heads, grimaced—or smiled—
Displaying their yellow teeth.
When they stamped away disgruntledly,
I saw in that white simplicity
How they had left clear field beneath—
Twinned, irregular shadows of green
Where stubborn flesh had been.

Young Snow

The three feet drifts
of the Overtoun Road,
black scribble of twigs for miles
balancing their thin white walls
in the fresh-squeezed light!
That day there were poems everywhere.
Blood-faced, stamping through
that creaking dazzle and that rare blue,
I laughed at the stains of steaming yellow
where the bellowing bullocks huffily
peed and butted and munched their hay.
In the Springside shop, dizzied by snowglare,
hunched old ladies in extraordinary hats,
clutching their wire-mesh baskets,
muttered, outraged, 'Is this no awfy, son?'
       And I agreed.

Blowing Out an Egg
aged 12

It was a ritual exercise in care—
to blow out a finch's or blue tit's egg,
transforming the patterned container of life
into the prize itself. First,
the pin-pricked hole in each end, then
holding it poised to your lips
with nail-bitten fingers and thumbs
like a miniature musical instrument
you were trying to gentle a note from,
pursing your mouth with precise pressure
to start the albumen's gossamer
lengthening into the toilet bowl. And after,
if the egg was fresh as it should be,
the pumping gold of what would now
be no singing bird, in small rich gouts
sinking through the water to the bottom.
And you'd flush that voice away.

Sacrifice

Opening the cardboard box that had held
a long winter coat for my mother out of the catalogue,
the ash-frail rows, arranged in sawdust,
from bough-cleft, twig-fork, thorn-bush, tussock,
were flooded with sterile day in their angular nest.
But to me they were beautiful,
my thick-freckled face pored over
each peppered, blotched, speckled or smudged or swirled
stopped beginning of a small bird's world,
in pastel blue and green, or white so pure
it seemed just solider light,
each airy husk a token of sorts
in the egg kirkyard of a schoolboy.
In those days, robbery was my form of love.

*Redpoll, goldcrest, song thrush, wren,
willow tit, linnet, skylark, dunnock—*

only my gaze then incubated them,
and all that hatched was possession's joy.

A Sparrowhawk's Nest

Which we never found, but the thought
of finding one was astonishing, talked of in hushed voices—
the big fierce rust-blotched egg in a sweating palm
on a doomy evening in the windy woods with a storm
crackling and me
miles from home in a torn jersey,
only excitement to keep me warm—
oh it was primitive! A sparrowhawk's egg,
a bartered death that said *I live! I live!*

The Herriers

Once, near dark, a football lobbed in the whins
landed beside a pheasant's nest
crammed with fifteen eggs, in a scrape in the ground
I found when I reached the ball.
I was astonished. I hadn't
seen such a nest with so many eggs before.
And we all got one, or more,
of the olive ovals more precious than gemstones—
sat round with our spoils, football forgotten.
So armies divide up the takings of war.
I went home in triumph with two eggs, my share,
as darkness thickened. Now what I see
is the female pheasant making
her delicate way, by instinct, back
under the spiny sprays to her fifteen eggs of air.

At Twelve

All the forbidden glimpses, the convex
greens or blues or whites, like the eggs
of blackies and thrushes and linnets
cored with blood and jelly,
was the hot uprush of spring and sex,
the girls as if they had given
a wisp of a secret away. . . .

And the helpless look of a hen blackbird,
glazed wide eye and beak and tail
terrored above the rim of straw among
thorns when our clamouring gang
flushed her in bursts of clucks, to thrust
our hot hands in.
It's the look I remember most today.

The Whitethroat at Hamilton Bus Station

A scraggy tree of improbable song
at Hamilton's crazy bus station,
fresh from Africa
to a Lanarkshire spring
set something off in the back of my mind,
over unnoticing faces.

I didn't acknowledge it yesterday; now
I feel I possess some secret code
(as others do, for other things),
identifying his rush of notes—
the lonely warbler claiming
one tree and a barren patch as his own,

optimist
over the fuming buses, and minds
preoccupied
though mine, perhaps alone,
gave him the briefest notice—
and passed on.

He's suddenly perched in my head,
hid on his twig in a quaking tree;
over girls with rings,
in the latest fashions
dreaming of weddings
and the settled lives,
he sings to me.

II

Light Up Lanarkshire

This public poem was commissioned by South Lanarkshire Council, who in 2006 developed a project, 'Light Up Lanarkshire', to light up at night various public buildings in the county, one of which was the Miners' Memorial in Cambuslang.

I

Lanarkshire's built of light, on light.
Before there were women and men and places
Dignified by names—Bellshill, Hamilton,
Larkhall, Cambuslang, Blantyre, Forth—
The ancient forests and ferns
Caught in their green cages
The travelling rays and locked them
Up like a miner descending day after day into dark.

And the ages passed. The forests passed, were pressed
Under huge tonnage of sand and silt, then buckled
By volcanic force into seams at different layers, all
Hidden from light of day,
Upper Coals, Ell Coals, Pyotshaw, Main Coals,
                Splint and Cannel,
Virtuewell, Kiltongue, Upper and Lower Drumgray,
For coals had their names as families did,
According to character and the depth
                at which they were found.

Coal is a terse black language
You could translate to the rustling tongues of money.
It is stilled fire. It is a sunbird locked in an ebony cage.
It is light made solid.

And light is magical, it cannot be tasted or drunk directly
(Though we drink and eat it every day),
It cannot be lifted, you can't fold it up like a blanket;
Clear, yet shone through a prism,
Is the luminous violet and red and yellow and lime
Of the born and broken from its brilliant beginning
That streams with ease across space to us, bounces around the world,
Acrobat of the spectrum, and the eye's reason.
Its truthful rays, indifferent,
Were locked in the black subterranean seams,
Where it slept for millions of years
Like some perversion of the fairytale princess
Awaiting the kiss of her lover.
While over its sleeping abundance, out in the upper air,
        everything happened,
Men were inventing, inventing, inventing.
The age of steam required to be fed
By the sleeper deep in her ancient bed,
Which invented the miner. So the miners came
And the greed of the landed—
Who owned, bizarrely, the light locked up underground
From a time way before there were owners of anything—
That was translated by sweat of these tough thrawn men
To money, to paintings, to genteel houses
And crinolines of ladies, to art, to society weddings,
To the sun of polite and gracious life—
Built, as always, out of the bestial sources.

II

So the Annals of Lanarkshire are the annals of light
Caught in its cage of coal as the miners were
In their thousands in this hard county, stepping out into the air
After nightshifts with blackened faces, white-eyed,
Like men on old film negatives, summer and winter,

Leaving the ponies, who could not be brought above ground
Without giving their eyes some protection,
As of souls, entering heaven.
And what did it mean, to mine? Often it meant
To lie on your side among glaur and water in a three-foot seam,
Hacking and hacking, with hundreds of feet
                of Lanarkshire rock straight up
Above your head for a ceiling. In 1910, 45,000 miners
Toiled underground in these Lanarkshire pits.
Many escaped into nature and kept
Whippets and pigeons, collected birds' eggs—
Flight and air locked up in a patterned shell.

James Cambridge of Mossend was one. He gazes, dignified, out
In his necktie and suit with his strong-jawed wife at his side
From this photograph propped among pens on my table,
In black and white and grey. He worked forty years
In twelve-hour nightshifts, six nights a week,
In Thankerton pit. His oldest son is my father.
I remember him only as a stern old man
White-chest-haired, in his long johns rising to pee dark amber
In the reek of ammonia into a pot he kept under the bed,
Or waving his walking stick at me,
All stubbly threat, from his big armchair
When I ventured near in his final years.
I was seven and so knew nothing.
He had been the head of a team, but never paid out
The wages to men in the pub—they would drink them,
Let whiskies and half pints light up their minds
In the ancient cave with its gantry.
They had to come round to the house
To collect their pay on Saturday mornings.

What hope kept these men going? Their children, perhaps,
Like my grandfather's daughter and triumvirate of sons,
And occasional gestures to something better,
Such as the time after drinking he spent too much
On a fancy clock for the house
And his wife gave him a sherricking.
He had the clock, wrapped up, in his hands and simply
Dropped it, onto the hard stone floor.
It sat, I was told or else have imagined,
Propped for years on the mantelpiece,
Hands stopped for good as if something had died
At that moment—some miner's urge toward betterment.
Now it is only a story, forgotten in dark like the mines themselves
Abandoned forever hundreds of yards underground, or flown
Like the young skylark my grandfather found
One morning in May or June with its eyes damaged,
Like his had been by gas attacks at the Somme.
He bathed the bird's eyes for weeks in diluted
Solution of Boracic powder, as he had with his own,
Till the lark, five inches of speckled brown feather,
A mote of wildness, could see again.
And he let it go, from the back wall.
Hollywood couldn't have dreamt up a better symbol,
Trite, profound, and true. And who he was really
His remaining sons don't well remember
But banter good-naturedly over
Which one among them was chosen to polish his mining boots.
For he always had to be spruce as a gentleman, stepping out
            for his evening shift.
Thousands of similar stories are lying in their rich strata,
Coal that will never be mined or reborn as fire—
Seams laid down in temporal heads.

III

So this is for lighting up Lanarkshire.
To light up a county is to have power
To take a piece of the sun and direct it,
It is to illuminate, to bring out of dark
As coal was brought by thousands of men,
Is a gesture against the great dark that awaits us,
Like the stars' punctuation of the universal night.
It is to create and to add, it is never subtraction.
It is the rose in the dandy's buttonhole, or
Like my grandfather's watch on an Albert chain,
Or scarlet Vespucci ink in a fountain pen. It is
To celebrate colour and gesture and rightful action.

So light up this county,
Let it blaze out at the throw of a switch and let
It celebrate the living and shine
In commemoration of the dead and their stories, gone,
Whose blood is ours, whose emotions are live in us,
Who spat out their soul in black dust on the paving stones,
Whose ossified lungs permitted clear skin and flowers in vases.

Remember them, when the lights switch on.

Light Leaves (1)

i

The night you tripped in Ayrshire,
(which marked the start of the end,
hurrying to take the chain off the door
you secured obsessively,
no matter how long
she was gone for,
and fearing her sherricking
as back from the Bingo she would have stood
bursting on the gusty doorstep), miles away

in Lanarkshire, unlocking my door I found inside
a robin flirt-fluttering
up and down, stopped
at the invisible wall
of one of my kitchen windows. And *Damn*
was my first thought, until I caught
its drumming-hearted weightlessness
in my cupped palms and let it go
at the kitchen door to all the unwalled air

of spring. And *Damn* was my second thought: *a wild
bird in the house is a bad omen.*
Old family superstition. A plethora of tales
of visiting birds and death. It had got in
through the letterflap stuck open by a sheaf
of half-delivered letters and, it struck me only later,
had simply been seeking a cleft to start a nest.

ii

This is a house of decrepitude.
The old cat buckling above her frail haunches,
fur-covered bones when I lift her,
like lifting a carrier bag of twigs,
empties her bowels on the living room carpet
unceremoniously, as my father
chunters on in some dismay
about twenty-four dead. 'In Pakistan!
Brendan, that's in Pakistan, not here!'
'Not here,' he says, considering, then:
'Poor ones in Pakistan.'
                              The brief
tabloid celebrity's distress on the front page
of the *Mirror* is his own, and something inexplicable
about the time his *Limit* watch is keeping
preoccupies him for hours. His wedding ring
is taken off and lost. When I leave
he sits up in his armchair and the old
cat twins him on the armrest. And you
let out a little laugh as we embrace,
and stand out at the door and wave, diminishing
until I turn the corner. All of us are marked
by this dark autumn evening, dry
leaves along the pavement in the streetlights' amber sodium.

iii

I shave my head to feel fit to face him
in his final days. Off it comes,
such as it is, below the buzz and minimising
steel of clippers lowering pitch
at every coarser patch. A kind of praise,
the lolling strands reduced to this suede fuzz
so near the bone. Now this is me
kneeling over the bath's white glaze
with the giant insect raining
in little clots the dark
filaments I love to see
onto the stark ceramic. This is me,
brother now as much as son in this shorn-bare
exposure to the judging sight and air—
fussless as mowing a lawn, the heft of skull
plain and solid as an iron hull.

iv

To get you up these horrible winter mornings
she only has to say, 'The bus is coming.'
The bus to the daycare centre. You think
you're going to work. And so comes back to me
every winter workday morning in the seventies,
the fifteen minutes till 6.40
religiously you'd take to drink a mug
of tea and read through yesterday's *Daily Record*
in the striplit kitchen silence.

And then without a word you would go out
and gun the Austin 1800 engine
impatiently in the spacefrost dark
till me and my uncle followed. An hour
to Inverkip. All this without a word.
Building a power station. The dignity of work etcetera
that thirty years later swings the white
wasted bony legs out over the bedroom floor.

V

It seems designed to guarantee longevity:
my father now, to whom I am
brother, nephew, no-one, must
inject himself with insulin twice a day,
rolling up his shirt to show an off-white
chicken strip of belly; and my mother,
helplessly needle-phobic from the one
stuck in the wallpaper she vigorously washed
half a century ago, that sank its silver length
completely among the tendons of her hand,
must take a nervy guess with her dried-up eyes
at the '14' on the gauge my father needs,
then leave the room as he, she hopes, injects
and tries to fit the cap back on the needle
in several attempts because his hands shake.
Describing this, I understand your laughter.

How laughable it is, this love in age.

vi

I take my father's blood, release the spring-clipped
needle into his proferred fingertip
and squeeze the swelling bead of worldly red
to sufficient size to dab it on the dipstick
inserted in the electronic gauge,
which beeps the fifteen seconds down to give
its reading, prognosis turned to numerals
but tenderly, another day in which to live
among these esoterica: Nathan, just seven,
pre-empting every sentence in *The Mask*;
renewing light of February in the living room;
my mother, reassured by family in the house,
in the kitchen washing plates and singing
scraps of hymns as if this were, already, almost heaven.

vii

Because the visitor had one
you had to have one, too.
Neither of those my sisters bought
seemed any use. You tossed them aside, astonishing
technology. And so it fell
to me to bring the most
basic model I could find, remove it
from the bamboozling
intricacies of packaging
and make it live, connect you
to the great buzzing circuits of the world

or such was the idea. Until
the week-upturning whim had passed, you kept
its helpless complexity below your pillow,
a lit line to your rescue, an escape route
to that Mossend you friendlessly wailed
to get back to, out of this stranger's house.

viii

My nephews are in the living room,
lively as a bunch of swallows.
Only their light can match your gloom
although it is December, and trick you
clean into self-forgetfulness;
until they're gone and in that afterglow,
unwilling crows, we sit around and wait.

ix

When you said, as you went off on one,
blowing through your lips,

'Phhh!—bloody hell, a snow-plough!'
at your wife's rough-love, exasperated

combing of the few remaining stalwarts
on your liver-spotted crown

I admired the unaccustomed flash of metaphor, and now
put pain into rhythm in its working out:

getting the snow-plough easily enough;
wondering about the snow.

X

My father's toy trains were his birds.
Down the years, as we grew,
the models got smaller. Finally
he was down to the smallest size they made
to fit the space he was left with. Mini-gauge.
Dainty wee things. Even I could admire
their fine engineering, their primary colours,
their unexpected heft for things so small.
Reassuringly solid. Round and round they went with a buzz
through the miniature land he'd fashioned, fitted
with little bushes, trees, and look—
drip this oil in the tiny funnel and the train
would puff out smoke! I find it here,
that made-up stab at a perfect world,
a destination of finished care.

Exposure

Shaving your head is to go bare
under the full hot press of sun
frying your baldy scalp; to stop
ducking and feinting behind your hair;
to buzzingly shear all adornment, all
ornament and frippery, present
straightforward you to the world.

It is to feel the caress of the sexy air, and see
your father staring back at you
from out in the winter night
in a travelling train's window. It is to aspire
to the plainness of nouns, to stop
time by pre-empting time, and the instant
absurdity of combs. It is to bow

your head like an old dog
for a lover to dome your brow
in her cool palms, knowing the bloody
pulsing brain beneath. It is
an attempt at honesty, a minor
variety of courage; to be
a hot thin soil for rain.

Anthotype

Light, the first maker,
  the last destroyer,
gifter of green fire,
  builder of ash,

sets the old face
  in the darkening forest,
sparks the young lips
  to the star's desire.

O keep me in dark,
  intact and inviolate,
or herry me out
  to the murderous rays—

no perfect crypt
  but the dazzling coffin
of the ferrying deaths,
  the brine of days.

An anthotype is a photographic image created using an emulsion of crushed vegetable matter. The image fades rapidly if exposed to light.

III

Christmas Oranges

Clementines—
this pile of votive planets
on the fridge-top,
caught in their nylon net.

Some
baggily-skinned, so
hooking a thumb
easily under, then
the whole skin off in a one-er; some
tighter, more
reluctant to be separate
from their hearts of sun.
(Danger of making a juice-sticky mess of those.)

Then breaking them open—
fragrance of orange on the tips of the fingers—
peeling away
like a plaster from skin
                              segment by segment
held up to this morning light
that's coloured the juice of an orange, each
segment veined like the petal of a rose—
to check for the shades of pips
in the cool translucence—
the thrawn wee buggers, the embryos

lavish with thought of perpetual groves.

Praise of a Winter Solstice

Because once, round then,
I read *Sir Gawain and the Green Knight*
in parallel versions in my Ayrshire caravan,
threadbare in hope, loving
the courtly story of the quest
through the stripped woods and their dropletted light.
I preferred the sun's wild note
to every glittery bauble—
significant as the crumb
in which whole bakeries could be assumed.

Minimalist

In the need for sparseness, such
subtraction one can take too far
as if there were, or something took,
a wry satisfaction in reducing much
to little. Some things, of course, are not
designed to be singled so—
say, flesh from bone, despite the pleasure
of the spine's increasing definition
under fingertips, as if one prized
that shining architecture above its dwindling
twin: like a careful archaeologist
revealing a Skara Brae
out of sand that meant its saving and its end.

Gorse in Middle Age

When you put on coconut butter at bedtime,
   it smells like a hillside of gorse in bloom.
      It is as if those miles I used to roam,

searching the tough dry spikes
   for linnet and yellowhammer nests,
      have come inside, and I'm

lying beside them here in the breathing room,
   as my hand cast over your ribs alights
      in the dark on your blossomed breasts.

Progress

Jeez, *The Diamond*! Mind in its loonge
(the public baur was aye too coorse a den
e'en fer scruff like us) we'd hae a pint—ten;
fowk focht, blethered, fell oot here, tried tae scroonge
a dram, a fiver. Snake Dubois'd cam in, ower trig,
toupéed, his latest lipsticked bint ahin,
auld Peter'd keckle et the thocht o sin,
an banged-up History gret in er fantoosh wig.

They've gutted it entirely; it's
for lunchtime diners now at napkinned tables
and sippers of chilled Zinfandel; and my face fits.
A made-up girl toys with her obscure drink
years away from those muffled Babels.
And I'm going to pass on that pint, I think.

In Irvine

Meeting Willie Black in the crowded mall—
all the May beeches dripping in this wet day
pushing its fences tight round the mind—
and the pith and salt of his Ayrshire Scots
is stepping through a door in a pan-loaf wall
to that world of old, unillusioned men
who know too the landscape I know best
but speak of it in what seems a truer tongue,
unemphatic yet fitted to each leaf and tree;
and I am a migrant visitor where
for centuries his kind has sung.
When I tell him I'm working at Lawthorn,
his brows gather up for a moment. 'Whaur?
La'thorn', he says with a quick recognition,
but the second time round his saying it
(not from deference it seems but politeness)
gifts the name to me.
                    'So Willie, what's the craic?'

'Did ye ken auld Quarum o Annick is deid?
Aye—a hert attack at the fushin.
His mither's steyin in the big hoose noo.
They'd a special plot dug oot fer Melvin
somewhaur up ahin the hoose,
but the dey he wis tae be buriet
they couldnae get the coaffin intil it, coont o the wat simmer;
fer it wis gye near fillt tae the brim wi watter;
they'd tae bail it oot afore the coaffin sailt aff lik a ship.'

How such tales please me in the hectic mall
jostling and bumping—to be once again
in that undocumented world of old Ayrshire men
through the door in the pan-loaf wall.

Find

    Here is Aristotle's lantern, each
fine bone that makes up the little basket
    like a paneless lantern of several sides,
first described by Aristotle, the mouth-parts
    of the sea-urchin. Eating's necessity
      sculpted to elegance
in the spine-stripped cask cast on the beach
at Portencross, a hammered form pressed out
    from the swaying, briny tons.

Aristotle's lantern. Aristotle's lantern, in the storm!

Shell Beach, Eigg

There is no sadness
in it. Shell shingle—

the crunch and crackle
under your boots

in the swash of tides,
a billion husks becoming

sand. And what I love
is the multifarious

abundance,
the sifting shift

in the sea's
dance

of these
miniature sculptures, this

cast up, ruined
city of the salty empires, such

sorted randomness
of patterned lime. Look—

that it will never
recur as now

is hardly a thought
for grief. Festival

of the brilliant changes,
a vivid cemetery

where no one mourns
for the shining massacre

of every tide.

Light Leaves (2)

i

Leaves I like,
    at least as much
for themselves,
    as they
shelter the simmering eggs in May
    from such
thieves as I once was, who preferred,
God knows why, the blown husks light as mind
    to their chirruping ends.
Here's to those soft and helpless guards.

ii

The leaf in its little inn is more
    radical than the greatest prophet,
opening its green door
    to the traveller in his coat

of blue. The leaf is female, letting
    the light enter
to strike for the root
    in the dark;

and the world's made new
    in the forge of its cells
that fangs are born of, and wild looks,
    and kisses, as quietly

the leaf makes love
    to the long rays
exuberantly dying.
    The world is the leaf's thrawn child.

Take-off

They are bibulous retired colonels
    with boxers' broken noses,
who happen to be cross-dressers, discoursing
    one imagines, in a tone
of languorous hauteur. Each neck
    is an Indian rope, to levitate
the head and exaggerated
    pink/black Roman nose,
when it uncurves, and straightens.

Pylons, in tropic feathers. Each
    stilts through lagoons
of brackish waters, sieving,
    turning the world on its head.
    And, when it flies—flared
wings of unbelievable
    DayGlo pink, and black—

The neck's rope weirdly stuck straight out,
    legs rigid, straight, behind:
like witnessing a Cessna
    crossed with a fashion model—
—squadrons of them—rise
    eye-wideningly and go,
lugubriously beating, stiltedly
    elegant as giraffes.

The Lesson

Half past nine on a grey Friday morning in December,
   Thirty bleary faces smudged with sleep still,
Me wittering on about natural history—till
    One wee boy's 'Haw sir—whit's that?'
      Scraping of tables—a flocking straight to the window.

'Keep your heads down now, you'll scare him!'
   Tall as the weans, it had alighted
At a culvert beside the classroom
   And peered in, alerted, its neck
     Upright. The gaunt and uncombed hobo visiting

From his simpler, immediate world. . . .
   One yellow eye met sixty children's, met
Books, jotters, computers, pencils, desks. For seconds
   There was a silence stainless as rays. Then someone
     Twitched, and the mirrored gazes

Broke, and it flapped up, like a greatcoat, dangling
   Legs. The classroom erupted
Back to its twittering spectra—
   'Whit wis it?' 'It wis massive!'
     A light encounter, in a dreich season.

Awakening

At evening, under the douse of the dew
Pebbles at path-edges gradually sprout fat fleshy feet,
Roll over, come alive: the silent ritual happens.

Walking a path, as the sun dips to coolness,
I recognise one at the tip of my shoe; and suddenly
Hundreds. Look—

Their whorled brown cases
The size of walnuts, scattered
Down the length of the path.

I kneel to the world at their eye-level—
A fleet of them stirring, out to their narrowed horizon! Some
Olive-green; some leaf-lime, tinily-stippled,

With glistening bodies satisfyingly meaty; some
Silently gliding over the pebbles to somewhere,
Nowhere; this one making

Tiny head-motions as it rasps with its delicate radula;
That one, curved improbably back on itself;
Three, fascinatedly crowding around a dead leaf.

O plump cuts pronged on a silver fork!
But not for me. I stand, careful now where I put my feet,
And pick my way

Tall as a tower among
This slow-motion ballet
Of gleaming flesh, eyes that are periods

Swaying on periscopes, these pebbles
        progressing mysteriously,
Graceful-solemn munchers and scrapers, this
Armada advancing in silence under the drench
        of the Vauvert dew.

Frog City

Vauvert, Languedoc-Roussillon

Out in the night here, every night,
far from the worlds of women and men,
under the stars of France, lies the croaking
city—listen! Their near, particular voices
off in the distance
blend to a constant stadium roar
horizon-wide at the foot of the sky,
a hundred thousand grenouilles
out in the egreted marshes
gloating in the glaur and spawn
that the daily grind of dodging
the beaks of kites and herons
is over, and now
for the dark's delights;

and the stars of France in the spring night air
wink with approval in their high elegance
for the frogs' bacchanalia
in the glutinous waters, their
miles-wide disco of amphibian music, their
Baby I can't get enough
                       of your love.

The Queen

There's something almost vulnerably human in the way
The wasp, below the wine glass I've inverted
To a clear cell on my kitchen sill,
In pauses between her quartering, combs
Out each long antennae with a foreleg—
First one, and then the other,
Like a girl teasing out her tats,
Holding the fankled strands between
A forefinger and thumb;
And suddenly back to waspishness
With blurring spasms of wings,
Antennae quiverings—
Scaling her cliff of glass on pricking feet.

I only want to briefly look at her.
She is a queen, newly awake from her winter sleep;
In the flex and pulse of her abdomen are stored
Ten thousand summer wasps, wasp dynasties
Down the perpetual light of centuries;
And she will be adored.
But, for now, she rests, her segmented antennae
Drooping and her jaws, so secateurish,
Slightly open, as she clings against her prison glass
With the disconsolate air of a scunnered spaniel
Gazing out, not even angling her plated face
When my gigantic head
Looms like an instant mountain into view.

It is Easter Sunday; she wants to begin
Her own fierce story of resurrection
Though they would kill her still,
Those bleak gusts of March
And that high, wasp-heedless blue.

Alight

You step from the front door to the gravel
yard, and dazzlingly there
they are, arranged
along the telegraph wire, twenty or more,
animated (it's a scene of some excitement),
shaking themselves in puffed up quivers and flurries,
or scratching the side of their heads with a blurring foot—these
you've never seen before, but recognise
instantly. They seem
less plumed than plushed in velvet—
bronze and olive-emerald, turquoise, cream,
each in cravats of unnameable yellow. All
balancing in the breeze. . . .

For a minute only. Now look at them lift and go
over your head in their fluting crowd—
where are they off to? Where have they come from,
these altogether lovely things
leaving you here with astonishment?

And, for the rest of the day,
you're lit by their velvet lustres,
that casual arrangement of brilliance
chirruping, in a line.

'Hearing Astronomers Speak'
for T

Hearing astronomers speak
I remember the lowering sun
is only our local star
shining through the window
on a winter afternoon,
each long fierce orange ray
fittingly strange, born as it is
from the death of other stars
on unimaginable timescales
in which some other consciousness
perhaps saw light make nothing of a pane
as mine does, now; and the sun's
going down is only the earth's
slow enormous whirling round, all
its bodies, cities, cars
massively curving into the dark
that sparks out constellations like the nets
of Christmas lights in Glasgow, though
not lit in celebration but
simply because they are—
multitudinous slow bees
in the hives of space for the mind's cold honey
that make me shiver and long
for your warm bare back
and your heart below my hand in bed, beating
steadily and more frail through these
ungraspable stellar distances,
and your face's star.

Stylophilia

A surprising number of pens
were, and are, called after birds:
the *Blackbird*, the *Jackdaw*, the *Swallow*,
the *Swan* that was top of the range
Mabie Todd made till the fifties
in colours various as the plumage of finches.
Pelikan. The sleek *Namiki Falcon*
with flexible beak in shining 14 carat, as if
the quality of implement meant
the peregrine flight of the words.

The inks, too, have a kind of poetry:
Invincible Black. Lexington Gray.
Bleu des Îles, in Carribean turquoise.
The star-containing *Bleu du Soir*,
Noodler's *'Bulletproof' Socrates*,
and *Coucher du Soleil*.

Retreat

    I have a green roof here:
fescue, buttercup and clover,
where the bees visit and Atlantic drops
       bow stem and petal
in the pewtery air; and in below,
having burgled my little block of hours,
   down haze-diminished streets I go,
      light with flowers,
to some who'd close their door on them
     and some who cannot know.

The Great Things

The difference here is space:
your sight gets used to searching horizons:
that speck is a merchant tanker.
Is that dot of a person tourist or local?

To step round the gable at noon is to be hit by a gust
from Iceland. The house sails like a ship through a squall
rattling the panes of crofts on the further islands
smudged below that massive black;
there's a single limelit field.

No child has been born here for fifteen years.
On the west shore
the whiskery congregation, silent, patched with orange, is
an arrested stagger of drunks with a backdrop
of cobalt white-flecked sea
in Atlantic wince-light of the blintering days.

This evening as I walk down the road to the phone
there are spreading gleams on the pewtery plain
to the east, as if some great beast with a roar might emerge
pouring like waterfalls. Down on that shore
Tommy Mackay's TV is on, from the daub
of light through his pane: *EastEnders*' far fantasia.
On the right as I pass, a meadow-spread back,
Netta waves out from the kitchen window
                where she washes the plates.
Five miles east she can see as I can, tiny down at the foot of the sky
and striped like a barber's pole or a mint,
drawing the eye right down to it,
North Ronaldsay's lighthouse, late-sunlit—
visibility that means rain. And in an hour,

while the island's windows wink to rectangles of butter,
the red and silent sun will descend
into the cavernous din of the west.
A brief exclamation of rose, from under the edge of space,
and a sudden gustchill grey.

Elsewhere the great things of the world will be taking place.

That Dusk

The whole vast west was a pink astonishment—
everything in the room was pink! Everything
answered it. Everything
was silent, yet it seemed
the room and all it held
grew animated, excited by that great, when all is said,
day's last exhalation at the world's edge.

In the bathroom, too, everything answered pink—
the white ceramic, the towels,
the bath and sink—
the whole house glowing and burnished!

It stopped me a minute, it plucked me out
of my everyday concerns to look
through the wide window at the skyline
bright and hushed, before, sure and slow
it faded, and the pink radiance left
wall and cup and table
and I could turn back without guilt
to my small matters.